HOW TO START A BUSINESS

A Beginner's Guide to Correctly Forming A Business, Incorporation, LLC and 501 (C) (3)

By: Professional Consultant, Felicia Jordan-Lee

Safe Haven Business Consulting Firm

Acknowledgements

This Educational Module is dedicated to Current and Future Entrepreneurs. You can reach your goals with the right information, you can maintain success where you're at now and looking to go in the future, step-by-step.

- *I am very grateful for my Pastor and Husband, Rev. Jesse Lee, Jr., of From The Word Ministries, for inspiring me to keep growing in my God given Gift to help others, my Son Kendall for always believing in me, My Mother Belle Jordan for pushing me to go further, Both of My Sister Tambra Jordan, My Brothers J. R. Jordan & Jonathan for constant Counsel and Consulting, My Spiritual Mother and Mentor Pastor Joyce Farmer and The Temple of God In Christ Church Family for always being there for me.*

About The Author

Although the Company was branded in 2004, Felicia's Unique desire to assist others in business began in 1999. Since then, Felicia has continuously had a helping hand in Social Service Programs, Economic Development Projects, Grant-Writing Proposals and Preparations of over $500,000.00, in Proposal Submission and Approval of Awarded Grants.

Felicia is known as the 501 c 3 Specialist, as she has carefully demonstrated her Passion, Professionalism and Success to her Colleagues and Community, in leading others in the right direction in Federal, County and State Registrations, to start a business.

Felicia continues to build the continued Legacy left by her Father The Late Bishop Willie Lee Jordan, Sr., in the For Profit Sector with Safe Haven Business Consulting, as new areas of implemented programs increase in the Non-Profit Sector serving and collaborating with other Organizations throughout the entire State of Illinois, Surrounding, Neighboring Cities and Counties, to educate all, is with her passion for business and economic development.

Introduction

In starting a Business, there are several steps that should be taken properly, to setup a business. A Business Consulting Company is to make sure that as you move forward in pursuing your goal, to provide the best of Business Solutions for you. Look for Tangible and Realistic Services, to help you get to the next level in establishing your business or moving forward in your existing business.

A trend that I saw in the early 1990's into the Millennial Years Starting in 2000, was that people wanted to quit their jobs to start their business. I thought was fascinating concept because many people who ventured in this manner into business were able to do just that and succeed at it, but they already prepared for their well being by saving money, using their pension to live off of, retiring and using their 401K's if they fell on hard times.

My point in saying this is that they had established a plan to succeed whether they work or the business bloom or not. If you are starting a business, until you are ready to financially take care of the commitment of the business and your personal care needs outside of the business, keep your income coming in. I would not suggest quitting your original means of support.

It's important to find time to do what you love and that's what I was able to do. I had a skill, my Father trained me in for years and now I'm no longer working side by side with him, but the wisdom and information he shared with me, I carry in my heart, especially when new and creative ideas began to flow. My success is defined by the things that are still growing in me to share with others.

Felicia Jordan-Lee

How To Start A Business
Step 1

- Select a name for your Business
- Perform a Business Name Search through your Secretary of State or through the Internal Revenue Service (IRS). This is done to make sure that the business name you are seeking to have, is not already in use by someone else.
- If in fact that there is someone using the name you're looking for, you can always keep the original name you wanted for your business, but add something onto that name or select a new name.

Felicia Jordan-Lee

How To Start A Business
Step 2

Determine what type of Business you will operate. Understanding your entity type, will help you to file the correct documents needed to be established and what is expected and what is excepted as either owner.

- Sole-Proprietor- is someone who owns an unincorporated business, receiving profits for one's own self.
- A For Profit Company- is formed to earn profits for one's own self
- A Not-For-Profit Organization- is formed to not withhold earnings or donations for ones own self, but to give to others that are in need.

Felicia Jordan-Lee

How To Start A Business
Step 3

After you have chosen the type of Business you will operate, determine if you want to Incorporate your Business and what type of Incorporation you'll be: (S Corp or C Corp, which present taxable differences)

- **A Sole-Proprietor Company-** Cannot be Incorporated
- **For Profit Incorporation-** a business established in your residing state allowing legal transferrable and limited liability business owners with creditors, state and federal governments
- **Not-for-Profit Incorporation-** A nonprofit corporation is a corporation formed to carry out a charitable, educational, religious, literary or scientific purpose
- **Limited Liability Company, (LLC).-** A flexible business structure for independent owners and shareholders of the company, where tax benefits are gained and legal protection of your business and personal assets.

Felicia Jordan-Lee

How To Start A Business
Step 4

- As this step is completed, you can file to obtain an Federal Identification Employer Number (FEIN or EIN). This number will identify that your business is registered through the Internal Revenue Service. This can be done online, or the form can be filled out and faxed in.
- This process can be completed online or forms can be downloaded from: www.irs.gov

Felicia Jordan-Lee

How To Start A Business
Step 5

Depending upon what type of entity created, Bylaws or an Operating Agreement need to be prepared for the company/organization.

- By-Laws for Profit Incorporation – Puts emphasis's within the business daily operations. What's expected of each party involved in the building of the company.
- By-Laws for A Not-for-Profit Incorporation- Determines how a charitable corporation/organization runs during the life term of founder or if voted out or if one has expired, all assets will not be kept for one's own self, but donated to another charity or the state in which it was established.
- Operating Agreement for LLC- Causes set rules to be in place for each shareholder and duration of the company or if the company or founder has expired.

Felicia Jordan-Lee

How To Start A Business
Step 6

- DUNS#-After completing proper steps for your Not-for-Profit Corporation, you should then acquire this number. The D-U-N-S Number is a unique nine-digit identifier for businesses. It is business credit file, which is often reviewed by potential business partners/sponsors to help predict the reliability and/or financial stability of the company in question.

To acquire A DUNS#, you can log onto:
http://www.dnb.com/

Felicia Jordan-Lee

How To Start A Business
Step 7

Only the Not-for-Profit Business Filing have other steps to be considered A Tax Exempt Organization and to be Exempt from State Taxes as well. After going through the initial steps of establishing a Not-for-Profit Entity you can:

- Download Form 1023 from the irs.gov website and Complete.

- Submit with the Application Requirements and Fee as suggested. Wait 3-6 months to hear of your determination from the Internal Revenue Service.

- A State Tax Exemption, which can be done online for free, cannot be filed until you have received your approval as a Federally Recognized Tax Exempt Organization.

Felicia Jordan-Lee

How To Write A Business Plan 1.

A Business Plan is needed to express your company's mission, vision and goal for existence. Letting your consumers know as a Professional Establishment:

- Who you are
- What you do
- What you will do for the future
- Why should anyone take interest in your company, become a partner, sponsor, give a private loan or donate in any way.

Felicia Jordan-Lee

How To Write A Business Plan 2.

- A Business plan consists of many components implemented within a company's instructional manual such as:

- Mission,
- Objective Summary
- Start-up Summary
- Services
- Market Analysis Summary
- Employee Handbook
- Budget, etc.

Felicia Jordan-Lee

How To Write A Business Proposal 1.

A Business Proposal differs from a Business Plan in so many ways. Unlike the business proposal, a business plan shares your entire intentions on your business, whereas a business proposal only shares minimal information to the person of interest such as:

- Auto-Biography/Portfolio of Owner/Founder
- Introduction of Company
- Current Activity of Services
- Futuristic Goals

A Business Proposal is also good for Marketing and Advertising.

Felicia Jordan-Lee

How To Prepare For Grants

Preparation for Grants takes place as you are actually preparing information for the grant to be submitted for reviewing, but haven't yet submitted the grant. BEFORE YOU CAN SUBMIT FOR ALL FEDERAL OR SOME LOCAL RFP'S/GRANTS/BIDS YOU MUST HAVE:

- EIN #
- INCORPORATION
- FEDERAL TAX EXEMPTION STATUS
- REGISTRATION WITH THE ATTORNEY GENERAL OFFICE in your State
- DUNS # THROUGH D & B (DUNS & BRADSTREET)
- REGISTRATION WITH CCR
- REGISTRATION WITH SAMS SYSTEMS
- REGISTRATION WITH OSHA
- REGISTRATION WITH GRANTS.GOV

Felicia Jordan-Lee

How To Write A Basic Grant Proposal

In my years of preparing grants, I have always followed the step by step approach that was given by the agency looking to give away funds. Grants are not guaranteed, it's a yes or no process, as there are others who could possibly be looking to apply for the same funding.

Here's a simple complete list to follow:

- Eligibility Requirements-Check to see if your organization fits into the criteria their seeking to fund
- Letter of Intent to Submit Proposal- Most times, funding agencies look for you to ask their permission to submit a full grant proposal, without it, they may not accept and tell you to apply next time.
- RFP/Proposal Deadline- Complete within a timely manner, submit several days ahead of time, especially with federal grants.

Felicia Jordan-Lee

Things to Know a.

- Processes can be completed online or by mail. For downloadable forms goto: www.cyberdriveillinois.com
- Mailing process takes up to 7-10 Business Days or more, after the application has been received by the Secretary of State, in the City you desire to do business in. Please be mindful that after setting up your business, Sole-Proprietors are required to register with the County in which they do business in.
- Most online processes takes approximately 24-72 hours

Things to Know b.

- If this step to complete the Federal Employer Identification Number is processed online, a FEIN is issued instantly, if done by fax, this process may take between 24-72 hours.

Things to Know c.

- A Business Proposal maybe presented upto a 1-5 page Document

Things to Know d.

- Missing any of the key steps could delay in Federal Grant Applications and Approvals. DUNS#, CCR, SAMS SYSTEMS and OSHA Registrations all take place after your Tax Exemption Approval Process, through Grants.Gov, which is considered the Main Federal Government Website to search for Grants. These are steps I'd suggest anyone to seek Professional Assistance.

Services Provided by Author

- **Felicia J. Lee is not an affiliate or representative for the Secretary of State.** Felicia J. Lee is A Documentation Preparer offering Non-Attorney, Non-Lawyer Services in the profession that she has a passion for as A Professional Consultant. As of December 2017, Felicia now holds a Bachelors of Science Degree in Criminal Justice-Human Services, A Licensed Notary Public in the State of Illinois, A Professional Tax Preparer through the Internal Revenue Service and will Graduate with A Master's of Science in Business Management in 2019.

Protecting Your Organization against Grant Scams

- Pay attention to words that try to lure you into believing something that is not true. Most Books that sell Grant information, will at some point and time expire. Grants are not always accessible after a certain season or the following year.
- Do not give out your personal information or send money to anyone.

Where Passion Build's the Vision....

Safe Haven Business Consulting, look forward to providing Business Solutions for you, to assist in your Vision, Dreams and Goals coming into fruition. We are A For-Profit Company that assist Communities and the General Public in several ways, with our Educational Materials and Seminars.

We offer Contractual Consulting Services to many and will continue to offer the best of our services, to the best of our ability. We look to Teach others how to properly set-up their business. Providing Tangible and Realistic Services to our Clients, is what we do to help you get to the next level in establishing your business or moving forward in your existing business.

Business Matters to serve For Profit and Not-For-Profit Corporations, FEIN's, LLC's and 501 (c) (3)'s, Business Plans and Business Proposals. Personal Matters, we Prepare, Power of Attorney Documents, Living Will and Last Testament Documents, etc.

Felicia Jordan-Lee

Reference

- corporation. InvestorWords.com. WebFinance, Inc. http://www.investorwords.com/1140/corporation.html (accessed: March 27, 2018).
- Non Profit Corporation Law and Legal Definition | USLegal, Inc. https://definitions.uslegal.com/n/non-profit-corporation/
- Nonprofit Food Bank Business Plan Sample - Financial Plan https://www.bplans.com/nonprofit_food_bank_business_plan/executive_summary_fc.php#.Wrq63nxPilw.twitter via @bplans

www.ingramcontent.com/pod-product-compliance
Lightning Source LLC
Chambersburg PA
CBHW051834210526
45473CB00005B/1878